Nature's Teachers

Wisdom from Animals

Madhav Thenappan

Made with ❤ on the BookLeaf Publishing Platform
www.bookleafpub.in
www.bookleafpub.com

Dedication

I dedicate this book to my cherished parents. A heartfelt thank you to my dear mom, an artist and hobby writer, for recognizing my talents and nurturing my skills. Your inspiration, motivation, and guidance mean the world to me. I am truly grateful for all your time and effort. And thank you, Dad, for always encouraging and supporting my endeavors.

Preface

Values are the cornerstone of strong, morally grounded personalities. Yet, in the rush of material pursuits, they are often overlooked. Like a compass, values guide us toward a meaningful and fulfilling life. But where can we find these lessons? The answer lies in nature.

The natural world is a vast, harmonious tapestry of creatures, each with unique strengths and roles. They coexist, contribute to the balance of life, and, in doing so, teach us some of the most profound lessons on character, resilience, and integrity.

This book presents a collection of twenty animal poems, where each creature speaks poetically of its virtues, inspiring us to embrace good values and positive traits. Values and good habits must be nurtured daily to become a way of life.

Acknowledgements

Thank you God for blessing me with talents, resources and opportunities.

Thank you 'World Wide Web' for the wealth of information.

Thank you 'BookLeaf Publishing' for providing a user friendly platform for self-publishing.

Nature The Best Teacher

Nature is a complex force that inspires
A world full of life - innumerable and diverse
Animals in many ways are similar to humans
They display emotions, social behaviour and intelligence
Lessons we can learn from the animal kingdom are
uncountable
Each creature plays a specific role and is accountable
They maintain ecological balance
And live in harmony with nature - one of the most
important lessons.
Animals are symbols of patience,
Empathy, courage, perseverance...
We must learn from their habits and behaviours
To better ourselves and the world of ours.

Assiduous Ants

We are tiny, but hardworking
The Queen - is childbearing
Soldiers - are patrolling
Some workers - are foraging
Few others - are nest-making
Together - we are accomplishing

Humans, work as a team - efficiently
Share knowledge and solve problems - innovatively

Brave Bear

I am a formidable creature gifted with physical prowess
I am strong, resilient and fearless
I endure hardships in the wild
Instincts and resourcefulness - my guide
I protect myself, my territory and my child
I face challenges; never flee or hide

Humans, be resilient inside and strong outside
Be courageous - confront challenges and fears
Power through and emerge victorious

Butterfly
The Resilient Beauty

I am a resilient butterfly
I overcame struggles to soar in the sky
Once in a cosy chrysalis
Undergoing metamorphosis
Pushing against the walls with might
I built my muscles for flight
And Emerged from the pupa looking bright

Humans, break free from the chrysalis of comforts
Challenge yourself and come out in flying colours.

Curious Cat

I am constantly observing, investigating and learning
Curiosity - a tool I use for surviving
I paw around searching for food and water
Scout out places to hide from my predator
I am a curious explorer

Humans, observe the environment with alert senses
Explore new spaces and experiences
Ask questions curiously
Learn and grow continuously

Chameleon
The Adaptability champion

I am a colour changing wonder
'Why' you may ponder

I camouflage for survival
Elude my rival

I warm up or cool down
Using my colours as a thermal gown

My colours of communication
Express my emotion

Humans, like me, you should adapt and grow
Embrace change and let opportunities flow

Patient & Clever Crocodile

I am an ambush predator
Camouflaged in the murky water,
I float passively
And wait for the prey patiently
When it arrives, I lunge and strike immediately
I drown it and feast happily

Humans, set realistic expectations
Watch for opportunities, exercising patience
Spot and seize the right occasions.

Devoted Dog

I am a devoted companion
I love selflessly without any condition
My owner's space I guard
For them I have great regard
Commands I readily obey
I am attentive and obedient any day

Humans, be present for those you care
Build strong relationships that wont tear
Form supportive bonds
And endure life's storms.

Empathetic Elephant

We elephants are gigantic
But have a gentle heart that's empathetic
When a member is hurt,
Others stroke its trunk to comfort
The herd slows down,
Matching the pace of the injured one.
We smell and touch bones of the dead
Displaying grief and respect for our beloved.

Humans, show compassion - build good relations
Empathise and strengthen social connections

Genius Gorilla

I am known for my intelligence
I communicate using vocalisations
Also express emotions
Through body language and facial expressions
I get past obstacles
Using my problem solving skills
I am a creative thinker
I use a stick to test the depth of water
And leaves to build my shelter
I exhibit social behaviour
And form strong bonds with others
I learn from my experiences
My memory is a big plus
I can remember locations of food sources
Can recognise humans and other creatures

Humans, be observant of your environment
Your memory recall should be excellent
Be socially intelligent
Tactically break through every impediment

Intent Hawk

My goal is to catch prey
From focus, I shall not stray
I see fine details with my sharp eyes
From 100 ft in the air I can spot mice
My eyes see a wide range of hues
I fly at high altitudes
And scan large areas for foods

Humans, view your purpose with sharp eyes
Let measurable and realistic goals arise
Examine opportunities and threats
Stay focused on your targets

Hippopotamus
'Self-care' Ambassador

I am a semiaquatic mammal
A self caring animal
I sweat blood red mucus -
A thermoregulator for a hippopotamus,
A sunscreen that protects me from the sun,
And an antiseptic that inhibits infection

Humans, take good care of your body
Sleep well, exercise and eat healthy
Calm your mind - be stress free
Inside out - be healthy
Feel good and help others happily

Conscientious Honey bee

We live in colonies
Made up of workers, drones and queens
Each of us have roles and responsibilities
We have earned the title 'Busy Bees'
Hives - we build and repair
For broods - we care
We collect and store food
Protect the hive from those who intrude
Our life span is short
But we accomplish a lot

Humans, dutifully play your role
Remember, you are part of a whole
Contribute responsibly towards the global goal

Efficient Kangaroo

In an arid habitat I thrive
Travelling long distances to survive
Tendons in my hind legs act as elastic bands
Allowing me to hop and do my errands
My tendons - shrinking and stretching
During take off and landing
Enable energy efficient hopping

Humans, build inner strength steadily
Spring back from setbacks swiftly
Work to overcome challenges efficiently
Leap towards success confidently

Lion The Leader

I am a born leader
The strongest predator
The pride's decision maker
A fierce territory defender
My group's caring protector
Roaring and purring - an excellent communicator
My intelligence makes me a strategic hunter
I set clear goals to be a survivor
I never give up - I am a goal achiever

Humans, be a charismatic leader
Your team, you empower
Be a goal achiever
And, your team's problem solver.

Flexible Octopus

I have a soft body
My eight limbs have amazing flexibility
My arms - bending, twisting and extending
Enable diverse ways of moving
Such as walking, crawling and swimming
My prey - I pounce and capture
I squeeze through cracks to escape from predator
I am an extraordinary survivor.

Humans, be open to learning and unlearning
Consider others' ideas and feeling
Be flexible and adapt to every situation
Survive and grow with determination.

Sagacious Owl

I can do a 270 degrees head rotation
Looking for prey/predator in every direction
I hunt in the dark using my sensitive hearing
My lopsided ears help in keen listening
I have binocular vision
That aids in depth perception
And helps judge the prey's location

Humans, examine different perspectives in every
situation
Keep your ears open for information
Discern what deserves attention
And make a wise decision

One-of-a-kind Penguin

I am a bird who is flightless
But nature has blessed me with uniqueness
I am an exceptional swimmer
Blessed with feet like rudder
Both ends of my body taper
A design to sprint underwater
Waterproofing oil my glands produce
Underwater friction it helps reduce

Humans, Identify and celebrate your uniqueness
Feel a sense of completeness.

Spider
The Web Engineer

I engineer cobwebs
For food, shelter and eggs.
Material and skill is all I need
I have got them in myself indeed

Humans, thrive on your asset
Just don't fret.

Methodical Squirrel

I am a pro planner
I bury nuts for having them later
I save for the cold months of winter
I store food by scatter-hoarding
According to nut type, I do grouping
To retrieve them, I use mental mapping

Humans, plan and organise to achieve your goal
Create habits, routine and play your best role
Improve productivity and attain success
Secure your future - save all resources

Tranquil Tortoise

My pace is slow and steady
My shell - a shield that protects me
I retreat into it when necessary
Slow breathing - my secret to longevity

Humans, withdraw from stressful situations
Anchor yourself in present moments
Breathe deep and root in inner peace
Mental turbulence will cease
Stress will gradually decrease
Progress step by step, in ease.